W0007589

What is your comfort zone (
Simon Lowe © 2022

Table of Contents:

This book was an idea that was created back in 2013 on a cold, wet, rainy afternoon. It started off as a slide presentation during a training meeting. In the beginning, it was never in my mind to turn it into a book and potentially help more people.

Creating this book was a step outside of **my** comfort zone!

Jim Rohn, the great speaker and mentor, talked about becoming successful not for the money, but for **who you will become in the process.** You can make money, and lose money, but when you grow personally in skills and confidence, you never lose those skills. You retain that growth forever, and those skills and the knowledge you have gained, will add to so many areas of your life. It all has a compound effect.

This is a **simple** book with examples and tools that you can use.

Acknowledgements:

This book is dedicated first of all to **Kevin Rider** – you were my first business mentor; all that you taught me will stay with me forever. You saw the greatest within me before I saw it myself. I will forever be grateful for this, from the bottom of my heart. THANK YOU.

I would also like to thank **Rie Pearson** for the inspiration you gave me to turn this into a book, and thank you to **Karen Cave**; my cousin, my sister and dear friend, for guiding me and helping with the editing.

What is a comfort zone?

We spend much of our life living within our comfort zone. It is said that 98% of the population stay within their comfort zones. At some point a comfort zone has different layers. Like an onion, and like people - we can peel back another layer.

Living in your comfort zone is all about what is safe and easy; you know the outcome. If you are afraid to take some risks and do something that scares you, you then run the risk of never really understanding your true self. When we are more open to taking on a challenge, we learn how to overcome our fears, and we understand ourselves more fully.

We find out so much more about who we are and what we are capable of when we take these risks; we find out what makes us tick and begin to see a different person deep inside.

When you start connecting with your true self, you open doors to change, growth, progress, love, and of course – an understanding that cannot be found **inside** your comfort zone.

Signs that we are stuck within our comfort zone

Here are a few suggestions that you may relate to:

- Things we are used to

- Easy

- What if I can't..?

- Lack of self-confidence

- Same old habits/ the 'habit zone'

- Fear

- Playing it safe

- "Just getting by" / "plodding on"

- Settling for less

- Procrastinating

- Others finding us predictable

- Turning down plans or ideas because of fear

- Making excuses

Reasons we may be stuck

We spend much of our life living within our comfort zone. We are creatures of habit, and we like to avoid anything that causes us pain, poses a potential risk, or makes us uncomfortable. There are things we are **used to**, and things we are **not used to**, and if we are lacking in self-confidence, then we may be affected by other people's opinions, especially if they are urging us not to do the thing that we are afraid of.

This fear could come from childhood; if you have been told by your partners or teachers that you are worthless or no good, and will 'never amount to anything,' this can have a real effect on one's self-esteem.

If you kept on being told this, the seed has been planted and you may continue to believe it; you may even believe that there is nothing you can do to change this belief. But if I told you I didn't grow up having role models; I grew up having people around that I **didn't** want to be like and seeing many situations I **never** wanted to be in – and this was valuable in showing me which way I wanted to go in life.

Not all of us are dealt the right cards. But that doesn't mean that you cannot reshuffle your deck and become the best vision of yourself.

Hitting rock bottom

Often it seems that this requires us to hit rock bottom before we can make changes - it really is NOT always required to make that breakthrough.

We get challenges in life, from job rejections to relationship breakdowns to health challenges. Perhaps instead of saying 'Why me?" we can look at it with a different question: 'What is this challenge teaching me and what can I learn from it?'

Or even: "How can this challenge lead to a better life?"

After all, we cannot fully avoid challenges in life; it doesn't matter how comfortable or wealthy or insulated we are from life's hazards. There will usually be something happening to test our patience, our peace of mind or our sense of safety.

Challenges in life happen all the time; we can **learn** from them or **run** from them. These challenges are here to test us, or maybe to push us in a different direction or show us a new path to take.

A SIMPLE EXERCISE ABOUT 'FLIPPING THE SCRIPT'

Take some time out now and ask yourself some questions about the obstacles in your life right now. Thinking about these ideas can feel very hard at first, but the more we exercise our brain 'muscle,' the more skilled we get at asking ourselves these questions and looking at our challenges **in a whole new way.**

It is all a matter of perspective. For example, you may be going through a very stressful event such as a divorce. It is normal to have a lot of very negative feelings about a challenge such as this.

Negative feelings may include:

- Feeling like a failure
- Feeling despondent
- Being afraid that you will never meet someone else

But if you turn this around, and start 'flipping the script,' you could look at it this way:

- You have become stronger
- You have become more independent
- You have left a toxic situation or one that was not making you happy

Consider these questions:

1. What challenges am I facing right now?

2. What are these challenges teaching me?

3. What can I learn from these challenges?

These issues may be very hard to think about, and that is okay. Learning to face things even when they feel hard or upsetting, strengthens our ability to solve problems and come out of our comfort zone.

Learning to answer difficult questions **honestly**, helps us conquer our fears.

It makes us less afraid of negative emotions.

It helps us build confidence in ourselves and our abilities.

If this task has been especially difficult to do, be kind to yourself and do something relaxing and enjoyable afterwards.

Ideas for how to come out of our comfort zone

How do we begin to step outside of our comfort zone? It is all about **challenging** yourself.

The first step could be to attend an event that will give you knowledge, understanding or inspiration.

Even if you are only taking small steps forward, you will get closer to what you want. Tiptoe if you must, but **take a step.**

In order to know what steps that you may need to take, it can be good to set down goals on paper, and then think about what the smallest steps are that you could take towards your goal.

Setting goals

It could be that financially you are taking some action to change your situation. For example, you may need to save £80 in a month so that you can go to an event that is related to your interests.

Saving that much money to attend one event could be a **BIG step out of your comfort zone!**

It could also be that **actually attending the event** is the big step.

To reach your goal, a solution could be the following, as a way of looking at expenditure and the simplest ways of saving money:

In the mornings before work, you go to the coffee shop and buy a coffee; you do that every day and on Fridays you get yourself a muffin as an end-of-week treat! You would have spent £20, and doing that over four weeks equals £80, so you could cut out the coffee shop visit and instead bring a jar of coffee to work with you.

Outcome: **You raise the £80 needed and achieve your goal!**

Giving up the coffee and muffin is a short-term sacrifice for long-term gain; going to that event could well change everything for you. It could lead to **further events** or **meeting new contacts**.

It could even create **momentum**, and a huge boost in **personal confidence**. I will talk more about events in another chapter.

Hell – giving up a daily muffin will also be massively beneficial to your **health**.

*

You may wish to build a business or a brand. This can require a lot of trial-and-error and trying new things which are maybe not comfortable to consider, especially if you are quite introverted or just not used to 'putting yourself out there.'

Stepping out of your comfort zone means to take action outside of your normal routine; that can feel uncomfortable but will help improve your situation. Changing your habits could be posting a short 2-minute video on social media, with you talking about the positive day you're going to have.

It is not just about influencing others – doing something like this will have an impact on you because you will get more confident at speaking publicly, at finding your voice, and at using social media technology in general. Also, other people are going to see your video and it will have an impact on them; it may push them to do something, cause them to feel more positive about themselves, or just give them a little boost - your video will be **inspiring other people.**

Never give up

I remember the first time I spoke on a team webinar; there were a hundred people on the video call. I was shaking the **first** time I did it, the **second** time I did it I got better, and the **third** time you could not shut me up!

I went on to host some webinars and do training on these calls. I even ended up going around the country speaking at events with rooms filled with people.

And this is somebody who was initially terrified of appearing on a webinar for a few minutes. It just goes to show how we can build confidence and get used to doing things that used to terrify us. We may even learn to enjoy and **relish** the things we once hated.

A healthy diet could be your step out of your comfort zone

This could mean switching from eating ice cream and chocolate to eating fruit and vegetables. It is not that ice cream is all bad, but over-indulging can definitely be bad for your health, especially if you are in danger of developing conditions such as high cholesterol and diabetes.

Coming out of your comfort zone could involve drinking more water, taking up exercise that you are not used to, joining a class, or simply **moving more**.

Getting healthier is never a bad step and can have a knock-on-effect on many other areas of our lives, such as socially, or with our confidence.

A personal story: how watching a video led to a whole new lifestyle and hobby:

I saw this video containing pumped up music, there were men and women exercising in a gym. I had not set foot in a gym for twenty years.

The advert went on to mention about learning boxing in *eight weeks* – joining a boot camp, gaining confidence, helping your mental health, meeting new friends, and raising money for a children's hospice. It showed clips from previous shows that been done, and it put a *fire* in my belly. I wanted badly to be involved.

I was looking for something to challenge me, as I had gone back into my shell. I had lost hope in myself, and I was unhappy. I was eating too much of the wrong foods; I was over-indulging in processed food and takeaways, and of course I was drinking alcohol most nights. I was doing all this as I was unhappy; stuck in a toxic relationship. I felt like there was no way out of this, and felt so much pressure on myself, just being with someone for the sake of it. I do **not** recommend this; it is **not** good for your mental health and personal well-being.

As I was going through all of this, I was also bottling up my emotions.

I would not talk to anyone about how I felt; I just blanked it all out and focused on the online business I was building up around my day job. I thought that was the only way for me to deal with everything.

I also started to train for the boxing event. It was very hard work.

But - I gained confidence, got fitter and stronger in body and mind, learnt to eat better, plus I made new friends through the boxing. It pushed me to another level; a **whole different version of me that I didn't think was possible.**

And you know what? I went on to box in that white-collar charity event at the ripe old age of forty, and I went on to do two further boxing bouts after. This was something I never could have imagined I was capable of.

It just goes to show how our whole vision for ourselves, and our life can change for the better when we try new things.

The boxing ring is not for everyone of course, but life is like a boxing ring: the ups and downs, the slips, the punches, having a plan for each round - everyone has got a Rocky story in them, and the ability to go defy the odds and **smash it.**

I don't tell you these stories to boast but to **impress upon you what can be achieved.**

The benefits of stepping out of our comfort zone

- Learning to act in spite of fear
- Embracing the unknown
- Exploring new things
- Going for your dreams
- Building confidence
- Choosing happiness
- Liking the changes
- Abundance
- Living without limits
- Fulfilment
- Getting the most out of your life
- Meeting new people
- Opening new doors for yourself
- Learning new skills
- Learning how to achieve happiness
- Inspiring others

These lists could be endless, the same as our comfort zone. Sometimes the smallest step in the right direction ends up being the biggest step of your life.

You don't have to take steps alone. The journey to self-improvement can feel like it might be a scary, isolated one, especially if you are moving away from familiar situations or people.

But one of the amazing things about doing and learning new things, is that often we meet new people, make new contacts, and open social doors for ourselves. We don't have to walk these journeys alone.

For example, taking up a sport or hiking could mean **teaming up with a friend**.

Joining a business group or network could mean **interacting with many like-minded people**.

Attending an event will put you closer to **potential buddies and contacts, opening doors for you.**

A real-life example of coming out of a comfort zone

The comfort zone, that wonderful place where we live a perfect life. No one can threaten us, no one can harm us. A state of complete bliss living within our own utopia.

For me the comfort zone was always a place I cherished. It kept me safe from harm. It meant no one could judge me. It meant my life kept on going the way it was going....

Being an online entrepreneur, my comfort zone was stretched and squeezed every which way, as I tried to keep inside it. What I didn't realise was the harm this was causing to my business. So, one day I told myself, "It's time to step out into the wide world." You see, the comfort zone in my opinion, is a state of mindset. Sure, you can stay in your "white picket fence" lifestyle. Or, you can take back control, open the gate and walk into the street and down the road.

When I decided to open the gate and take that first step, I didn't quite realise how quickly I would start my sprint down the road! The more I ran, the stronger my mindset became. Fears I once had, were wiped from my head. If I could take the first step, why would I stop?

And this is when the magic in my entrepreneurial journey began. Starting from scratch and knowing nothing, I built a business which has hit $2million in sales turnover. I have made connections from around the globe, on every continent. I frequently feature on live calls and presentations to hundreds of people. And in the background, now thousands of people know my name.

Not bad for taking a single step.

So do something today your future self will thank you for. Get out of your own way and take that first step. I can assure you, the journey down the road will be well worth it.

- Eddy Lamb, Network Marketing Professional

A GOAL SETTING EXERCISE

We've talked about comfort zones and reasons for taking steps out of them. Now let's set a couple of goals; to keep it simple, we'll begin with a short-term one and a long-term one.

You may wish to set the short-term goal first, as it may be easier, seem more achievable.

Or you may wish to set the long-term goal first, and use the short-term goal as a 'stepping-stone' to get there.

The two goals could be related, or for completely different areas of your life. There are **no limits** when it comes to how many goals and dreams that we have!

Short-term:

This could be to read a particular book, or to attend a particular event, online or in person. It could be to look up some information, to buy a particular item related to a passion or goal, or to adopt a new habit. It can literally be anything towards improving yourself, your future, or your happiness. It can be as small as you like.

Anything! Go for it! **Write down that short-term goal here**:

Long-term:

This could be a larger goal, one that's a little further in the future. It could be something like a dream career, or business goal, or financial goal. Something that requires more time or more steps to be taken towards it. Your goal should be personal, about **you** and **your happiness**.

Write down that long-term goal here:

Creating a vision board!

A vision board is a visual collection of pictures, cuttings, photographs that you find inspiring. It could also be inspirational phrases, such as your favourite quotes. You can place these on a corkboard or a large piece of card; they can literally go anywhere: on a wall, on the fridge, on your computer screen.

For example, goals can be people you want to meet, gigs you want to attend, places you want to travel to, an income goal... You could also have books you want to read, the house you want to live in, the car you are dying to drive, social medial platforms you want to master, how many followers you want.

Goals can also be creative: a book you want to write, a book you want to read, things you want to create.

There is literally no limit to your goals and your dreams when it comes to your vision board. You can keep adding and expanding as much as you like. There are no rules to how you inspire yourself:

Consider also: family, lifestyle, or spiritual goals.

Visions for a new job, the next stage to your career, or the next level in your business.

How to create vision boards

The best way to start is to grab a load of magazines and catalogues, make a drink, get yourself comfortable and start to cut out anything that grabs your attention. Once you have done that, you can then arrange them on the vision board, in any way you feel will jump out for you.

Place your board somewhere around your home that catches your attention. This will be a constant reminder to you to go for your goals!

There are so many stories where people have done this, developed their visions which have then become a reality. It has happened for me, for many others, and it can happen for you.

Other mediums

Create an audio message to yourself telling yourself where you will be in six-months-time or even in a year. Create for yourself that verbal vision, whatever you want. Play the audio to yourself every day, and this will help keep you focused. Hearing your own voice reciting your goals is a powerful boost.

Create a mind movie, a digital vision board: get all your photos of goals, with inspirational quotes mixed in. Put them all together on slides, make a short video. You're in control, **you're** the director.

I have made a few videos myself, and included my goals, inspirational quotes, people that I want to meet. I also have past achievements and goals that I have crushed, in order to give me that reminder that I **can** do it.

Remember: we all have dips in life, but it's in the dips we grow. It is during the challenges that we learn, make changes, and find new solutions to problems.

Carry your goals around with you in a notebook that fits in your bag, or even have small cards that fit in your wallet or purse, this will give you reminders that it is always good to look at your goals every day.

Find ways to go and experience your goals in small doses, if it's that supercar you want, go and book that Red Letter Day - get a photo taken with your dream car and put it on your goal board.

Cars might not be for you, there are plenty of other experiences out there, so go and find one that puts goosebumps on your skin and excitement in your belly.

It may be that dream family home - go and book that house viewing, visualise yourself and your family living there, get a photo of you all standing outside your potential home and use that for your goal board.

When you yearn for something, put it on your goal board. Having your goals and dreams visualised is much better than having them rolling around your head like marbles. **Do something with them! Give yourself every chance to achieve them!**

Write yourself a large cheque and put it in your wallet or purse. You may be thinking, *why do that?* If you have not heard the Jim Carrey Story where he wrote himself a cheque, I would highly recommend checking it out – it's on YouTube, an amazing story.

If you go onto your play store or app store on your smart phone, there are many different types of free and paid video creator apps. You can add some upbeat music to it. If you're having a down moment, this will fire you up.

You can make all different types of mind videos; a few examples could be for New Friends, Social Life, Inner Peace, Loving & Appreciating Yourself, Vibrant Health, and Wealth Abundance.

(Space for notes):

(Space for notes):

Our comfort zone doesn't just have to be about our career

We have comfort zones in all areas of our life. If you think about how we tend to live as humans, how many habits we have that we follow day to day, from the breakfast cereal we choose to the routes we take by car or on foot, to the clothes we wear and the people we interact with, much of how we do things is within our comfort zone.

Humans by our very nature, dislike change, but we also do need a bit of uncertainty, a bit of variety. As the saying goes, 'a change is as good as a rest.'

This is why in British culture we love a holiday. They are designed to be a complete 'break' from our day to day lives and routines. But even holidays can become part of our comfort zone, especially if we always go to the same place, do the same things, and eat the same foods!

Here are some other areas of comfort zones that are worth considering:

- How we parent
- Our mental health
- What we do for fun
- Health and fitness
- How and what we eat
- Hobbies
- Our self-confidence / assertiveness
- What we wear, our hairstyle, make-up
- Our friendships and relationships
- Our intimacy habits
- Our travel habits
- How we decorate our home!

Why does it matter so much?

What are the risks if we never bother trying anything new? Well, it might mean that we are not living life to the full.

It could be that we are giving up the possibility of not being financially comfortable, by **not** pursuing our goals or making a change.

We might realise how much of life we are missing out on, by **not** pursuing that goal of a happy relationship, or a more fulfilling social life.

Or it might simply mean that we are not living freely and having as much fun as we could be having!

Imagine going through your whole life, never embracing change or taking a risk.

How will that feel at the end of your life?

People at their end of their lives rarely regret a **full, interesting life.**

They only regret all the things they **didn't do**, and the chances they **didn't take**.

Don't be one of those people…

AN EXERCISE ABOUT OUR COMFORT ZONE

Have a moment now to think about your comfort zone and answer these questions.

Really think about what you feel safe with, and what you could be giving up if you don't push yourself a little in the **areas that matter**.

Don't just answer them - **write them down below: it will mean more and have more of a powerful impact on your commitment to achieving them.**

In what areas of my life am I feeling particularly stuck in my comfort zone?

What could my comfort zone be costing me?

What is my alternative if I don't take action today? What could I be missing out on?

What steps am I going to take to come out of my comfort zone?

(Decide on at least one small step for each area that you are particularly stuck in and want to make changes in.)

Inspire yourself: Be in control of what you put in your head

What do I mean by this? I'm talking about reducing the daily habits that are **not benefitting us**, and replacing them with **more helpful ones**, i.e., habits that strengthen us and bring us closer to the person we wish to be.

I set a personal goal for myself five years ago that I would not watch the news when I first got up in the morning. Because it can set you up for a negative start to your day. **Instead**, I would watch a **positive video** on YouTube and read five pages of a **personal development book** each morning.

It is amazing what that does to you: it sets you up for the day, and gets you in that positive mindset before you leave your home in the morning. Beginning your day with **positive intent** seems to help things flow better, and can even open doors for better things to come your way.

Learn while you're walking or driving

When I'm walking to work in the morning, I listen to a personal development audio on my phone. Spotify and Audible are a brilliant source of these.

If you are driving, instead of having the news on, why not listen to audio: turn your car into your own private university! You may not pick it all up because you are concentrating on driving. But your subconscious mind will pick up some of what your conscious mind does not.

Learning at home

I have always got something inspirational playing at home. True stories, biographies, tales of adversity, and people who have conquered insurmountable odds to become successful. Even if I'm in the middle of cooking or pottering around the house, I may have audios playing or be playing some positive stuff on YouTube and letting it run.

Never underestimate the cumulative power of what you allow into your brain every day.

Here is a quote from the great Tony Robbins: "Garbage in – garbage out!"

There is nothing more incredible than hearing people talk about how to do the very 'thing' you want to do yourself – **and realising that you yourself can achieve it too!**

I listened to and got inspired by so many podcasts that I got curious about how easy or difficult it would be create one myself. I looked on YouTube and found some 'how to' videos. I created my very own podcast, this proved to me that you don't have to be famous to have a podcast. Anyone can start a podcast and talk about what they are passionate about.

I am passionate about helping people, and interviewing people who are passionate too. **So, this is what my podcast is about.**

You can find my podcast on Spotify - search for my name **Simon Lowe:** my podcast is called **Create Your Own Destiny.**

Creating your own podcast

You don't need any fancy equipment to get started - just a standard smart phone, or your iPad or laptop.

There are many great videos on YouTube where people are showing others how to start a podcast. Find YouTubers that you like, and follow the guidance they give. You may have to watch several videos, but who cares? This is FREE guidance, and it can be invaluable.

Think about what you are passionate about, what you **love** to talk about. Your show has not got to be perfect; if what you are offering has value for people, then that is what matters. Don't wait or compare your content to others until you are 'perfect,' or it may never happen. Growth comes from mistakes and from learning!

Every creator goes through a learning curve over time. Focus on **progress, not perfection**.

*

If you too want to get a podcast up and running, go over to **Anchor -** you can do it all on there for free. That is just one platform you can use, there will be many others too. Go create!

What is stopping you from creating your own podcast or YouTube channel?

Some tips for motivation and organisation

1. **Plan your week** - on a Sunday evening, block out times you are working or needing time for study or research. Goals are important, and so it is important to **carve out some time for working towards them.**

Don't forget family time. And time just to 'be,' this allows your brain to refresh, and can give you some of your best 'ideas' and 'daydreaming time.' Music or walking in nature can be particularly helpful for this too.

You can use Google Calendar, or if you prefer to have a paper version of the week, use a paper diary or calendar, showing Monday to Sunday.

2. **Have a 'To do' list.** It is always best to make this list the night before, and start off with the highest priority to the lowest priority tasks. As you tick these off throughout the day or week you will get a strong feeling of satisfaction, which will boost your confidence.

It could be that a top priority goal is a **baby step** towards a **larger** goal.

We will talk more about goals in another section.

3.Read ten pages (a good minimum) of a **positive or motivational book**; if you can't do ten in one go, then do five in the morning and five at night.

4.Watch a motivational video on YouTube or something that is **meaningful and positive for you**.

5.Write down things that you are grateful for; it could be the simplest things in life like your **morning coffee**, the **roof over your head**. Also be grateful for the **good people** you have in your life. If you do not have good people in your life, then **finding some** would be a good goal to set for yourself.

6.Look at your goals each day. It is good to reflect, and reassess.

7.Meditate. This may not be for you, I felt the same for many years, but try it as you never know what might 'click' with you. It does not have to be **classic** meditation; anything that helps you relax and find your 'flow' can be classed as mediation. This could be **sitting in nature** for ten minutes, **gardening**, or **writing**.

8.Consider and write down, '**What are my wins for the week?**' These can be anything you are proud of, from getting dressed and facing the day, to sending an important email, or applying for a course. Your wins are very personal to you, and important as they help you realise that you can achieve, and move forward with goals, no matter your circumstances.

9.Consider, '**What can I do better?**' This is not criticising oneself, but simply reflecting on your week, and thinking about different solutions to problems and achieving goals. Or it could be something you need to do **more** of (like drinking more water) or **less** of (like 'doom-scrolling' through the news.)

10.**Having an accountability partner**. This can be anybody who supports you and will be your 'cheerleader.' It can be helpful to **share goals**, and it is also great to have somebody give you positivity and encouragement when you make progress, or help pick you up if things are tough.

It is great to be self-motivated, but **no person is an island**. We **all** need social connections and emotional support. We **all** need to feel that we are cared about, and that we belong.

11.Join a book club. I have been with one for many years now; I get an inspirational book in the post once a month from **www.knowledgeisking.co.uk**

12.Follow people that you are inspired by.

A real-life example of coming out of a comfort zone

Stepping out of my comfort zone pretty much had the biggest impact on my life of late.

Stepping up and out led me to new ways of thinking, appreciating myself and others more, but also led to opportunities that just wouldn't have presented themselves if I had stayed where I was.

The extremely successful people I've met have passed on such knowledge and advice. The experiences I've had, travelling the world, are mostly thanks to the generosity of such individuals.

But ultimately, it's the confidence I've gained by stepping out of my comfort zone and mixing with such individuals that has helped me grow in stature and confidence. It has changed and shaped me to become the person I am today, and that is something I'll always strive to pay forward.

Anon.

AN EXERCISE FOR SELF-MOTIVATION AND INSPIRATION

Think about how you like to learn and enjoy media; do you prefer reading paper articles, watching YouTube videos, or listening to podcasts / talking books?

Scribble down some ideas here:

What steps can you take to expose yourself to positive media daily?

(i.e. setting an reminder on your phone to watch a positive video whilst you are making lunch, or go for a walk and listen to a podcast)

Write some ideas here:

(Write any ideas here)

Self-esteem: Your 'past self' does not define your 'future self'

If you let the past rule your future, then you are selling yourself very short...

Let me tell you a bit about my story, and why I am so passionate about personal development.

An unhappy childhood

As a child I was a victim of serious bullying, at school **and at home**. I was being told *'You're no good,'* by the people around me that were supposed to be **looking out for me and caring for me**. It affected me a lot. I saw and experienced things that no child should have to go through.

As a child I had buck teeth, 'National Health' glasses, hand-me-down clothes from neighbours... The pressure I felt at school, when I got bullied for wearing a classmates' old clothes - it takes its toll on you. *Every day, I felt like a lamb being led to the slaughter.*

Children can be so hard on each other. They are all still learning, but they never know what is going on behind closed doors.

I was around people who I did not want to be like, but! I had no choice as back then I was too young to do anything about it. I had no support around me. That negative seed was planted in me from a very young age.

That seed starts to grow, and you believe what you are being told, as you are being told lies by your peers and people you rely on to care for you. As you are living in that environment, you believe that is what is **'normal.'**

Even when it is far from that.

Now, thank goodness, things are very different for me. I broke ties with toxic people as soon as I could.

I started building **positive habits** and relationships with **positive, supportive** people.

What started to turn things around for me

The years of bullying: they had a knock-on effect. I did not believe in myself, and I went down that road of working jobs that I did not want to do, using drugs and alcohol as a way of blanking out the past, blanking out my feelings.

But I was **not** successfully blanking it out; I was actually reliving it day after day, week after week, year after year. I was reliving it by abusing and hurting myself, hurting my prospects, hurting my future.

It was not until my late thirties that things started to change for me; I joined a home business company, and was introduced to **personal development.** I started to interact with and surround myself with positive people. I heard their stories and where they come from, and found I had mentors - people who believed in me before I believed in myself.

I never thought that joining a home business would change everything for me. It began to give me a vision for my future that I had never considered before. It taught me to believe in myself, and I learnt the following things:

1. I started looking at myself differently.

2. I started gaining some confidence.

3. I learnt that you can't change the past, and there is no point feeling ashamed of it or burying it, but you **can** change the way you look at it.

4. I would not be the person I am now if I had not experienced the things I had.

5. **Anyone** can improve themselves, no matter where they are starting from.

A real-life example of stepping outside a comfort zone

The comfort zone. You know the one. That gentle tug into procrastination and safety. Routine boredom topped off with a tinge of guilt for being a lazy turd. A situation that we all need to be keenly aware of.

The problem with that safety is just that; it's safe. All of our immediate needs are met but none of our long term hopes and dreams are being built towards. My remedy to this has always been to find a task or skill and jump in the deep end. Put all of your fears and anxieties on show for all to see.

Last year I entered one of England's most notoriously difficult marathons on a whim. I had been running more routinely and had a goal to run a half marathon every month of the year. That rapidly became my new comfort zone. The half marathons had become routine and somewhat easy.

The marathon itself was a terrifying prospect but not as terrifying as the preparation. 16 weeks of structured training where procrastination was not an option. Just like that; a plan of action to work towards a goal with constant and measurable growth. No comfort zone and the measurable improvement kept me motivated to stay out of that nice but useless place. 16 weeks later- marathon complete.

My advice to anyone is to charge headfirst into a task no matter how impossible. You have the fortitude to conquer any of your impossible dreams if you will the practice into a habit. Yes, there is no comfort with this method... only growth.

- James Collings

A POWERFUL EXERCISE FOR SELF-BELIEF

Get yourself a blank piece of paper and start with these words: **I am ......**

This is going to help you think about who you are, how you see yourself, the qualities you like about yourself, and perhaps about the qualities you would like to work on.

See if you can get to 100 - I'll start you off... use the blank sheets provided:

1- I am healthy

2 - I am wealthy

3 - I am looked up to

4 - I am respected

5 - I am secure

6 - I am worthy

7 - I am ...

8 –

9 –

10 –

('I am' answers):

('I am' answers):

Yes, you **can** do this, you may want to do it in blocks of time, as it may take a bit of practice to think about yourself in positive ways. I believe in you, that you **can do this.**

If you are really struggling to think of positive 'I am' statements – it can be helpful to think of people in your life who like and support you. It could be your child, friends, a family mentor, anyone you feel accepted with.

Get a friend to fill in some of the answers for you!

Put yourself in their shoes, think about how they might see you!

For example, your best friend might see you in the following ways:

1 - I am kind

2 – I am Funny

3 – I am generous

4 – I am good at having fun

5 – I always see the best in people

6 – I always do my best

7 – I am determined

8 – I have beautiful blue/green/brown eyes

Don't be afraid to ask the people that you trust what they think your best traits are! Often, we have a blind spot when it comes to seeing ourselves positively. You might be surprised what people come up with!

We might be really good at dealing with conflict, or we might have a calming manner. We might be brilliant at making decisions quickly.

It can take time to see ourselves how others see us. Learning to do this can be part of **coming out of our comfort zone.**

If you have a child or a young family member who looks up to you, put yourself in their shoes. You may have a niece or nephew, and to them you may be their hero!

1 – I am a superhero

2 – I am positive

3 – I am fun to spend time with

4 – I am fun to go have ice cream with

5 – I am good at teaching life lessons

6 – I always offer to help with homework or life problems

7 – I give good advice

Different people may see different sides of you – positive and negative! And that is okay – none of us are perfect. We should focus on the **positives** for the purposes of these exercises.

(Page for notes):

Fun ways to come out of your comfort zone!

What are the types of things or events you could consider doing to come out of your comfort zone? Here's a few you might want to try. Sometimes, the crazier, the better! These types of things can be **great fun**, **build character**, and **boost** your **bravery**.

They could even lead to **better habits** and **fun hobbies**:

1. Tandem Skydive (especially for charity, a great thing to do)
2. Wolf Run - you could do this with friends
3. Race for life
4. Do a charity white-collar boxing event
5. Fire-Walk
6. Get your face painted
7. Organise a Macmillan coffee morning
8. Dye your hair! Or shave your head!
9. Encourage a child / family member to get involved!

There are just a few examples here, but each one of these could lead to other amazing things by taking that step. It is also a fantastic way to help your community.

What an amazing way to **lead by example** and be a role-model for younger children or peers.

The importance of attending company events or general success events

These are the places that are really important to go to; it is where you will spend time with people that lift you up, inspire you and make you feel good. We all go flat at times, and we need to recharge; after all, you would not let your phone battery go flat. So why let yourself go flat?

We all need things to look forward to, things to give us a **boost**.

I still remember going to my first company event; I went kicking and screaming, but afterwards, I felt so inspired and uplifted from seeing normal people achieving amazing things. I had that belief instilled in me: *if they can do it, so can I.*

So, if you are involved with a home business and your upline or sponsor is speaking to you about attending an event but you're not particularly convinced, **go anyway**. Go with an open mind. You cannot underestimate the power of these events. **You just never know** where it might lead you.

You also get to spend time with other like-minded people. I had many fun nights out - work hard / play hard too! There were also so many opportunities to pick the brains of other successful people. For the price of a pint or a meal it is worth its weight in gold, and you can get so many invaluable and important nuggets of wisdom and advice that can serve you well for years to come, just from **one conversation**.

From my experience, it was like being part of one big happy family, everyone wanting to help each other and cheering each other on. Some, you will be friends for **life** with.

Generic events / Success summits

(Personal-Development, listening to speakers and successful people etc.)

Generic events are slightly different, as they are not about one specific company, and you have different people from all walks of life attending. Everyone may be going for different reasons, but the atmosphere can be **electric**, and you can all feel really **united**. It can give you such a buzz, a new lust for life and for setting new goals.

I remember my first generic event I went to; an incredible **15,000 people** came together for a four-day Tony Robbins event in London, that culminated in a fire-walk. It was intense and exciting.

The whole thing absolutely blew me away. It changed everything for me. If anyone has lots of 'whys' or needs some serious uplift, then this event is for you. You may walk in there feeling as small as Tom Thumb, but after those four days, you will walk out of there feeling like the **Jolly Green Giant!**

*

If you look for the UPW (Unlock the Power Within) events, you may be shocked at the prices for the tickets, but one of my first mentors said this to me: 'Think of the value you will be getting, not the cost. You are going to meet new people on the same level as you and above - you will be able to inspire each other. You can meet that one person who could change your life for ever; this could be your future life partner or business partner, or that person who gives you that essential nugget of wisdom that means that **life will never be the same again.**

*

There are many smaller events you can go to, which are one or two-day events where you have a selection of speakers; these events are sometimes called summits or success events. Throughout the pandemic, many public speakers had to change their usual way of delivering talks, and do online events, and this was all new to them. **Successful speakers have a comfort zone too.**

They had always done public events, in person to perhaps a few thousand people in a room or hall. They had that taken away from them; they were in **their** comfort zone delivering in person and having a few thousand people calling their name.

Then the world pushed them in a different direction when they had to do online events. The same went for personal trainers, dance teachers, musical performers and artists. When life changed the goalposts, **many had to adapt**.

In life you are given challenges; these are here to test us. You can be within a comfort zone at any stage of your life, even if you are on top of your game.

I have even noticed previously relatively 'unsocial' celebrities putting out much more immediate 'live' videos in the wake of the pandemic – reaching out and being more 'immediate,' and connected with their fans. Perhaps even superstars like Sly Stallone and Arnold Schwarzenegger have been coming out of their comfort zones recently when it comes to social media!

A real-life example of coming out of a comfort zone

I've always been averse to sports and exercise, right from when I was a child. I didn't even like football, watching or playing, and the few instances I did try to play, I looked like a stick insect. Supple as a board, and very unfit.

When a friend suggested we take up running, I was 32, my heart sank. I couldn't think of anything worse. Olly was all too keen though, so I agreed to it. We practised on a field at the back of his house. Then he was like, "Hey, let's hit the road."

We jumped from running less than one mile, to running through sand dunes, up dual tracks, climbing the steepest hill after two or three miles of sweating, breathless, before finishing on a downhill. Roughly a four-mile trip.

It killed me. So much so, on the final uphill I felt close to collapsing. Every time. Little did I realise I had asthma, and that this was why. It didn't get any easier with practice, and I was always lagging by a good distance.

I came to dread the words, "Are you coming?" But I kept soldiering on, it was Olly who lost interest in the end.

The adrenaline gave me a buzz afterwards, and to finish without stopping midway was an achievement in itself for me. One of my demons had gone.

- Henry Johnson

How to set S.M.A.R.T goals

When you set your goals, it helps to make them **SMART**. Here's how:

S Specific - make your goals specific and narrow for more effective planning.

For example, rather than saying, 'I want to lose more weight,' you say, 'I want to lose a stone and reduce my body fat percentage by 5%.'

M Measurable – decide how to track how you are doing; what evidence will show that you are making progress, so that you can revaluate when necessary.

For example, you could note down when you lose your first pound, and every pound after, until you reach your goal.

A Attainable - make sure you can reasonably accomplish the goal within a certain time frame. Break it down into smaller goals if needed. The sense of achievement is what is important here!

R Relevant - your goals should align with your values and long-term objectives. Is the goal truly important to **you**? Is it something that matters to **you**? If so, **why** is it so important for you?

It should be something that is a **burning desire** for you.

T Time-based - set a realistic, ambitious end date, for task prioritization and motivation. We respond much more urgently when we have a deadline!

Strengths and challenges

To prepare for goal setting, it can be useful to seriously think about our strengths, and our challenges, so that we can figure out how we are going to bust through the obstacles that may be in our way. It is good to see these things as a part of life, because no matter how successful a person may be, they will always have challenges to figure out, and strengths and skills they can draw on.

I have inserted a couple of examples to give some ideas:

My Strengths are	My challenges are
1 *I am good at helping people*	1 *I do not have much spare money at the moment*
2 *I am determined and hardworking*	2 *I am in a job that I dislike and want to change*
3	3

4	4

(Space for more ideas):

Brainstorming goals

A goal I will achieve is:

.

To achieve this goal, I will approach the following people who can help or guide me…

1.

2.

3.

4.

These are some things I can do to help me achieve my goal:

1...

2...

3...

4...

My signature...

Name..

Date ....

Why not get your children involved too in setting their own goals?

Looking back now, I wish I had been taught this skill as a kid. Children are so imaginative, and they have no fear; you ask any child to write a list to Father Christmas, and look at the stuff they write down.

Tell them: You are a superhero, and will reach your goal!

(Space for goal writing):

Real-life stories by people who came out of their comfort zones

Remember to be strong and DO, because you never know who you might be inspiring!

Great things are waiting for you just outside your comfort zone. To prove it, here are some more real examples of ordinary people coming out of their comfort zones and demonstrating the amazing ways it developed them:

The lone parent

I've had a home-based business for so long, I cannot remember exactly when I started. I was always in full time employment, but as a single Mum of three, money was still tight.

We live in a coastal town and my children are active and always learning. Have you any idea how much a kayak costs? So, I needed an additional income just for their hobbies.

I decided, although I will say "No" to my children, when necessary, it would never be because I couldn't afford what they were asking for. Having no money was NOT going to be part of my children's upbringing. One of my non-negotiables!

During this time, I joined a networking company. Many people poo-poo these companies and don't see them as "real businesses." To be fair, I've encountered some stories when uplines (the people bringing in new people) have delivered some dreadful training and this leads to some dreadful practices which leads to allegations of spamming etc.

But for me, the ability to earn another income, with a flexibility around my family and job, was just amazing.

Back then, my upline ran a weekly training event online. Each week, someone from the Team would do a ten-minute training slot.

One week, a guy called Simon was delivering the training. He appeared to be a quiet and shy man. A bit nervous (who wouldn't be? He was publicly speaking in front of over 100 people, albeit online.)

I listened to Simon as he went through his presentation, then he said this...

"What is your Comfort Zone costing you?"

Wow! Light bulb moment!

In business, you have to put yourself out there. As an introvert, that's hard for me. But my mission was clear: I needed a kayak, a piano and the ability to travel with my youngest, football fanatic kid!

You see, Simon was right. Without being out there and open with business, nothing changes. And if nothing changes, we are stuck in our uncomfortable, just-over-the-bills, worried, squeezed and miserable comfort zones.

That one short sentence, changed my whole attitude to my business. Even years later, when I was about to press "send" to publish my first book, Simon's voice was in my head, "What is your Comfort zone costing you?".

What's the worst that can happen? People don't buy your products or services. So what! Someone else will.

Get out of your uncomfortable "comfort zone" and make life happen!

Thank you Simon Lowe. You Legend!

- Rie Pearson

The eleven year-old child

There have been multiple times in my life where I have come out of my comfort zone, but there is one in particular that I would like to discuss. I remember clearly, it was last year on one of my school class trips; Drayton Manor Theme Park.

It was a very hot day, and everyone was sweating from the heat. However, this did not stop a single student from going on the rides; in fact, it probably made them more excited. There was one ride that I was determined not to go on. The Pirate Ship.

I remember my best friends at the time trying to convince me to go on. They kept saying that they 'would go on it with me', or that 'I would enjoy it, honest!' Eventually, I caved, and went on with one of my best friends and my ex-girlfriend, while my other friend watched from below, staying with the teacher.

I still remember watching someone drop their shoes at the peak of the ride, splashing into the water below. If anything, that just made me more excited - I had lace-ups. We all sat right at the edge of the boat, me in the middle, my girlfriend to the right, and my best friend to the left. It was probably only a five-minute wait, but it felt like forever.

It was AMAZING. Despite my glasses nearly falling onto the person opposite me multiple times, and all three of us nearly throwing up afterwards, I begged to go on again. However, we had to move on. I know now that I will definitely go on if I come across another similar ride, and I now try things that I wouldn't have tried before.

- Ellie

The mother turned business owner / novelist

I always wanted to write, since I was a child. I tried writing a novel when I was about eighteen, but it was a disaster, and I gave up.

After I became a mother and had run a business for a few years, I gave the writing another stab. I had written a bit of poetry over the years, but nothing more. This time I was in my mid-thirties, and I didn't try to create pure fiction. I based my ideas on some kind of truth, made it feel real, wrote in my own 'voice.'

It began as a few disjointed anecdotes, gradually joining together into a narrative, and over the course of six months or so, I worked steadily and regularly on my book. I still didn't really know if I could *write* though, if I was good enough to put a book together, if anyone would want to read it. Would I get laughed at? **I had to try.**

My goal was to create a funny, adult novel, and make it believable. I did research into my subject matter, and into self-publishing, as I wanted to release the eBook on Amazon and do a good job of it. I had never done anything like this before, and I watched a lot of YouTube videos, plus I found a short 'how to' eBook which gave me the very basics to get started with.

I massively underestimated how much work creating a mid-sized novel would be. But I was so passionate about achieving my goal and getting my book out there, and that passion kept me going. I worked solidly and steadily for around six months, as it found its form and structure. I discovered that I got more work done out of the house, and regularly holed up in corners of my favourite coffee shops with my laptop.

I also realised that over 50% of the work wasn't the writing, but the editing, proofreading, changing around and re-editing!

They reckon that it takes 10,000 hours to become good at a new skill. I have no idea how many hours it took to create my book – from initial notes to typing up, checking and rechecking, edits and re-edits, to correcting any mistakes, to commissioning a book cover, uploading to Amazon and filling in all the relevant information including creating the 'blurb' and marketing info, deciding on the price etc. Plus of course SO much research!

Creating a book from scratch was the hardest creative task I've ever completed, and in fact one of the toughest things I've ever done. I'm very attention-deficit and get easily distracted. Finishing my book took blood, sweat and tears, but it was worth all of that because there is no feeling like getting that email from Amazon telling me that my book was now 'live' on Kindle. Just incredible.

Because of that first leap out of my comfort zone, doing a task I kind of thought impossible, I discovered a new-found passion for creating and publishing. It almost became like an addiction, but a happy one! It also built my confidence in myself hugely.

I went on to write and release five books in total, including a self-help paperback, with more in the pipeline. I also write experimental short horror tales on Vocal.media under the name Karen Cave.

I'm now learning how to create my own ebook covers, and have also helped others create and edit their own books. I've recently been working on a funny book with my daughter, who herself is an amazing writer.

My advice for if you want to write, is: **find what you are passionate about, and just get writing.**

-   Karen C (pen name: Eva Jean)

The actress

What I am about to discuss is highly likely the same for everybody, but I just remember how terrified I felt about doing something that I saw others seem to do so easily and effortlessly, and not give a second thought to doing. I felt so worried about it, and it was such a big thing for me to do, so out of my comfort zone that I wouldn't do it.

Every time I managed to do it a little bit or sometimes do it on an even larger scale, I would feel a sense of achievement. Now whenever, I do it, I enjoy it. It isn't too much of a problem. I am secure in knowing I will be fine.

I also know that if something happens to make it not go so smoothly, then I will be fine anyway. I had to go through huge anxieties and fear for me to see this though. How I saw it was just doing it!

What was it? What was so simple but for me was such a huge hurdle, that after doing it I wouldn't do it again for months and months, in the beginning, probably years!

Catching the train. Taking a train journey.

What if I get the wrong train? What if I get lost? What if I get kidnapped? What if I miss my stop? What if the ticket man sees I am on the wrong train? (But I HAD to get that train because I missed the last train and I NEEDED to get the train home to safety) What if...? What if...? What if...?

Of course, the last example only happened because I already experienced the mishap, to know of it. If the train man did come along my acting skills helped me a lot, along with my pretty and innocent looking face. I felt so deceitful, especially when I started purposely doing it to save money.

However, nowadays, I don't feel the genuine fear of being on the train anyway to pull it off. It is a good feeling having the money to pay for the right ticket always.

Being on the train is now a part of my comfort zone. Kind of. Depends on the journey. However, if there is some anxiety there, I always know that I will be fine. The anxiety is never too intense that I can't find something to do to relax and take my mind of off it.

In the beginning I would sit there frozen in fear, using my acting skills to make it look like I was just staring out of the window.

If something happened unexpected during the journey, like having to get off early and get on another train... the panic sent through me was intense.

"Just ask someone," again using my acting skills. "What will I say? Is this the train to (destination)?"

"Take a deep breath." My dad's words would sound in my head. I would take a deep breath.

"Is this the train to (destination)?" Would repeat in my mind over and over until I found a suitable target I felt OK to ask.

"Is this the train to (destination)?" Either it would be the train or they would direct me to the correct one or they would say "no". If it was a "no" I would just have to find a staff member. They would always direct me correctly and eventually I would be sat back down, staring out the window, frozen in fear again. This time with new thoughts, "please show me a stop I recognize, please show me a stop I recognize!"

Sometimes there would be the information over head, the writing of each stop the train would stop at. I just had to make sure I didn't drift off into another world in my mind and miss the stop.

However, if I did the miss the stop, I learnt it wasn't too scary just getting off then getting on another train back. The more mistakes I made the more I would stay alert not to make the same mistake.

How did I manage to get out of my comfort zone and make it into something I do without too much thought?

I had good enough reasons WHY I wanted to do it.

At first when I was a teenager, I would catch the train with friends and not pay much attention. Just follow them like a sheep and let them be my guide. My want was to be with my friends.

When I was alone and having to go on long journeys it would be to see family. They would have to map out the route for me to follow and meet me at the other end.

When I started going to London for acting work, no one was to meet me at the other end. I was always afraid I wouldn't find the place I had to be at.

I remember my first time on a professional set as an artist. It was an unpaid extra role for a music video.

I got off the train at the right tube station and walked. Hoping it was the right direction. I walked past someone who looked like they were waiting for whoever. I walked past them at first in fear of being wrong and looking like an idiot, then I found the courage to be brave and turned around repeating the sentence I was going to say... I didn't even have to say it. They asked me. I guess my bright multicoloured sparkly dress looked like the beach party dress costume they might use in the scene. I nodded.

Getting into acting and being on set at different locations and finding my way was super hard. I would feel so mentally exhausted but like I had achieved so much, that I wouldn't look at applying for any other unpaid work for a long while. Each and every time I got out of my comfort zone was confidence building for the next time.

I wouldn't have been able to have ever done that if I never got out of my comfort zone and made myself get the train alone, even if at first, I did have to get family to meet me at the other end and to plan out the journey for me.

Getting help with all of that is a thing of the past. There are always taxis at train stations and hopping in one and giving them an address is super easy, if needs be. I have learnt how to use Google maps now too. I have learnt to trust it. Sometimes it takes me a longer way round and round in circles, but I see it as getting in extra exercise and as long as I reach my destination eventually, I am super fine.

I have learnt however scary something seems to be, if you just do it, you learn that you can do it but also you learn that you can do even more things after learning to do that one thing. Once you learn and even make mistakes but continue anyway, you learn from those mistakes. Nothing has to be perfect.

Like the old saying, "as long you try," it sounds so simple but it's true.

Anon.

Thank you for reading

Thank you for reading What is your comfort zone costing you? I hope you were inspired to think outside the box, and that you are ready now to step out of your comfort zone. Remember: **tip-toe if you must, but take a step.**

If my ideas have resonated with you, please take a moment to leave me a review on Amazon / Goodreads. **Reviews are so vital for us new authors!**

To connect with me on Facebook, visit my page:

www.facebook.com/Si.lowe.coach

I would love to hear stories of how this book has inspired you, and where your journey has led you so far.

For more inspirational content, head over to Spotify for my podcast: **Create your own Destiny.**

See you on the other side of your comfort zone!

Si

Read on for extended written goal-setting exercises and journal!

(Space for notes):

A weekly journal to help you stay on track

Here's an exercise to keep you on track and help you reflect on your week. By completing each week and being consistent, you will soon see **results**.

At the beginning of the week write down your **priorities** and what you are **grateful for**, and the end of the week when you are reflecting on how your week has gone, write down your '**wins**' and what you feel **you could do better.**

Filling in this journal will help you stay positive and focussed on your goals and progress!

Week 1 Date

This week's priorities	I'm Grateful For
This week's wins	What can I do better

Week Two Date

This week's priorities	I'm Grateful For
This week's wins	What can I do better

Week 3 Date

This week's priorities	I'm Grateful For
This week's wins	What can I do better

Week 4 Date

This week's priorities	I'm Grateful For
This week's wins	What can I do better

Week 5 Date

This week's priorities	I'm Grateful For

This week's wins	What can I do better

Week 6 Date

This week's priorities	I'm Grateful For
This week's wins	What can I do better

Week 7 Date

This week's priorities	I'm Grateful For
This week's wins	What can I do better

Week 8 Date

This week's priorities	I'm Grateful For
This week's wins	What can I do better

Week 9 Date

This week's priorities	I'm Grateful For
This week's wins	What can I do better

Week 10 Date

This week's priorities	I'm Grateful For
This week's wins	What can I do better

Week 11 Date

This week's priorities	I'm Grateful For

This week's wins	What can I do better

Week 12 Date

This week's priorities	I'm Grateful For
This week's wins	What can I do better

Week 13 Date

This week's priorities	I'm Grateful For
This week's wins	What can I do better

Week 14 Date

This week's priorities	I'm Grateful For

This week's wins	What can I do better

Week 15 Date

This week's priorities	I'm Grateful For
This week's wins	What can I do better

Week 16 Date

This week's priorities	I'm Grateful For
This week's wins	What can I do better

Week 17 Date

This week's priorities	I'm Grateful For
This week's wins	What can I do better

Week 18 Date

This week's priorities	I'm Grateful For
This week's wins	What can I do better

Week 19 Date

This week's priorities	I'm Grateful For

This week's wins	What can I do better

Week 20 Date

This week's priorities	I'm Grateful For
This week's wins	What can I do better

Week 21 Date

This week's priorities	I'm Grateful For
This week's wins	What can I do better

Week 22 Date

This week's priorities	I'm Grateful For
This week's wins	What can I do better

Week 23 Date

This week's priorities	I'm Grateful For
This week's wins	What can I do better

Week 24 Date

This week's priorities	I'm Grateful For

This week's wins	What can I do better

Week 25 Date

This week's priorities	I'm Grateful For
This week's wins	What can I do better

Week 26 Date

This week's priorities	I'm Grateful For
This week's wins	What can I do better

Week 27 Date

This week's priorities	I'm Grateful For
This week's wins	What can I do better

Week 28 Date

This week's priorities	I'm Grateful For
This week's wins	What can I do better

Week 29 Date

This week's priorities	I'm Grateful For
This week's wins	What can I do better

Week 30 Date

This week's priorities	I'm Grateful For
This week's wins	What can I do better

Week 31 Date

This week's priorities	I'm Grateful For
This week's wins	What can I do better

Week 32 Date

This week's priorities	I'm Grateful For

This week's wins	What can I do better

Week 33 Date

This week's priorities	I'm Grateful For
This week's wins	What can I do better

Week 34 Date

This week's priorities	I'm Grateful For
This week's wins	What can I do better

Week 35 Date

This week's priorities	I'm Grateful For
This week's wins	What can I do better

Week 36 Date

This week's priorities	I'm Grateful For
This week's wins	What can I do better

Week 37 Date

This week's priorities	I'm Grateful For

This week's wins	What can I do better

Week 38 Date

This week's priorities	I'm Grateful For
This week's wins	What can I do better

Week 39 Date

This week's priorities	I'm Grateful For
This week's wins	What can I do better

Week 40 Date

This week's priorities	I'm Grateful For
This week's wins	What can I do better

Week 41 Date

This week's priorities	I'm Grateful For
This week's wins	What can I do better

Week 42 Date

This week's priorities	I'm Grateful For

This week's wins	What can I do better

Week 43 Date

This week's priorities	I'm Grateful For
This week's wins	What can I do better

Week 44 Date

This week's priorities	I'm Grateful For
This week's wins	What can I do better

Week 45 Date

This week's priorities	I'm Grateful For
This week's wins	What can I do better

Week 46 Date

This week's priorities	I'm Grateful For
This week's wins	What can I do better

Week 47 Date

This week's priorities	I'm Grateful For
This week's wins	What can I do better

Week 48 Date

This week's priorities	I'm Grateful For
This week's wins	What can I do better

Week 49 Date

This week's priorities	I'm Grateful For
This week's wins	What can I do better

Week 50 Date

This week's priorities	I'm Grateful For

This week's wins	What can I do better

Week 51 Date

This week's priorities	I'm Grateful For
This week's wins	What can I do better

Week 52 Date

This week's priorities	I'm Grateful For
This week's wins	What can I do better

The goals I have achieved this year:

1

2

3

4

5

A treat I am going to buy myself:

....
......

What will I do better next year?

My highlights of the year:

My personal Growth	Relationships

Health & Fitness	Family & Home

Books I have read/discovered or audios I have listened to	Events I have been to

Skills I have improved on	Things I would like to learn more about

Printed in Great Britain
by Amazon

23489742R00059